Published by D1 Productions LLC
www.d1productions.coach

ISBN: 978-1-7365362-6-1

Hi there, Ocean Explorer!

We're so excited to go on an adventure with you! Meet Finn the Dolphin and his good friend, Coral, your friendly guides through the ocean and beyond.

We love to explore, learn, and help others, and now we're here to help you become a confident and smart responder—both in the water and in life!

Finn is super fast and loves to race through the waves, while Coral is wise and always knows how to stay calm under pressure. Together, we'll teach you how to stay safe, keep a cool head, and make quick, smart decisions when it matters most. Whether it's learning how to escape a rip current or how to respond in an emergency, we'll be right by your side.

Are you ready to dive in? Let's explore, learn, and have some fun!

Let the adventure begin!

S STOP

O OBSERVE

A ADJUST/ALLOW

R REFRESH & REFRAME

1

Ocean Adventure Journal: What's Your Favorite Beach?

What's your favorite beach?

What do you love the most about it?

_____

_____

_____

Draw a picture of your favorite beach here:

Why is fresh air and being outside important for our health?

_____

_____

_____

2

The SOAR Strategy Escape Challenge

"I am caught in a rip current. Can you help me get back to the beach?"

Thank You for saving me from the rip current!

Now you are ready to become a "Resilient Responder"!

What would you do first if caught in a rip current?

_____

_____

_____

3

Ocean Patterns: Find & Draw!

Finn and Coral love looking for patterns in nature. The ocean is full of beautiful patterns—waves, shells, and even the ripples in the sand!

Look around your surroundings. Can you find a pattern?

☐ YES   ☐ ABSOLUTELY!

Find somewhere you can sit for a few minutes outside. Find some natural objects with patterns, it can be a leaf, clouds, bark on a tree, or even on a bird or a bug. Draw some patterns you see:

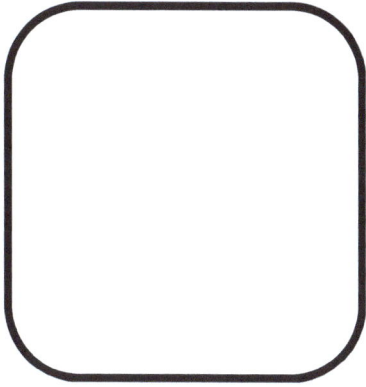

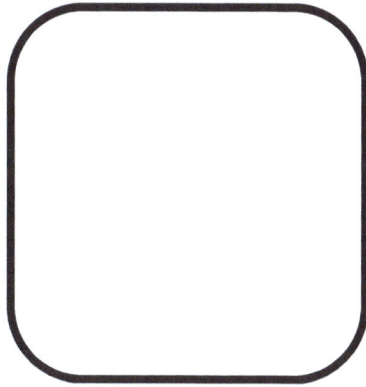

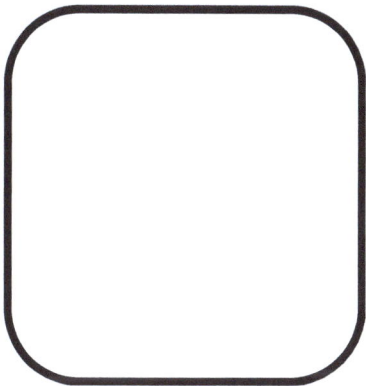

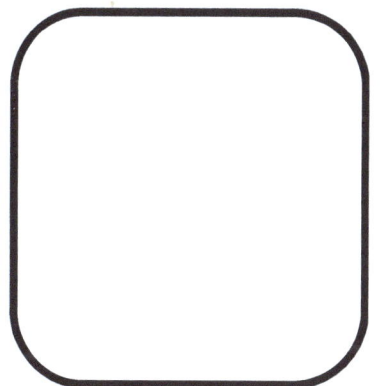

Just like nature has patterns, our minds do too!
What's a happy thought you want to think more often? Write it down!

_____

_____

_____

4

The Power of Water: Breathing & Calmness

When you swim underwater, do you notice how quiet and peaceful it feels?

That's because focusing on your breath helps you feel calm and strong. **Try this!**

- Breathe in deeply for **4 seconds...**

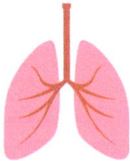

- Hold your breath for **4 seconds...**

- Breathe out slowly for **4 seconds...**

*Do this a few times. Now **HUM** when you breathe out!*
Humming keeps the water from getting up your nose when you are swimming under water.

5

Saltwater & Energy: Wash Away Worries

Did you know the ocean can wash away negative energy?

Let's do a fun exercise!

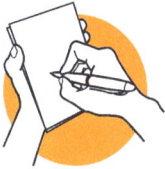

- **Write down a worry on a piece of paper.**

- **Put some salt in a bowl of water.**

- **Now, put the paper in the bowl and let the salt water soak up your worries.**

Bye-bye, worry!

6

Waves of Thought & Patterns of the Thinking

Your brain is like the ocean floor. Just like water carves patterns in the sand, your thoughts create pathways in your brain!

Use your finger to draw wavy lines in the sand or draw some lines on paper.

Think about a good habit you want to build, like being brave or kind.

Repeat it to yourself: "I am strong like the ocean waves!", "I shine bright like the sun."

7

Story Time: The Adventures of Finn & Coral

One day, Finn and Coral met a little fish named Sandy who was caught in a rip current!

Fill in the blanks:

- **When Sandy got pulled away from shore, the first thing she did was _ _ _ _ _ _ _ _ _ _.**

- **Finn and Coral told her to stay _ _ _ _ _ _ _ _ _ _ and _ _ _ _ _ _ _ _ _ _.**

- **To escape, Sandy swam _ _ _ _ _ _ _ _ _ _ instead of straight back to shore.**

- **Sandy also had to _ _ _ _ _ _ _ _ on her back and breathe when she felt tired.**

- **At the end, Sandy felt _ _ _ _ _ _ _ _ _ _ because she learned to stay calm, call for help, float, swim sideways, float some more, and then swim back to shore.**

Suggested Answers : *Call for help,* calm & float, sideways, rest, strong

- *Remember to call for help & swim with a buddy & near a lifeguard*

8

What Floats?

Check the objects that float and cross out the ones that sink.

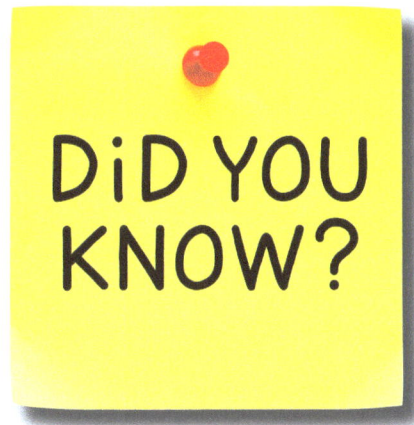

Your body can float, and knowing how to float can help keep you safe in the water.

Here's how it works:

1. **Big Breaths Help!** – Take a deep breath and fill your lungs with air. This makes your body lighter and helps you float better!
2. **Body Type Matters** – Some people float more easily than others. If you have more fat, you float better. Muscles are heavier, so strong swimmers might need to work a little harder to float.
3. **Saltwater Helps You Float!** – Floating in the ocean is easier than in a pool or lake because saltwater holds you up more.
4. **Stay Relaxed** – If you stay calm and spread your arms and legs like a starfish, you will float better. If you tense up, you might sink!

Draw a picture of yourself floating on the water:

9

Ocean Waves Relaxation Activity

- **Lay down and close your eyes.**

- **Imagine you are floating in the ocean.**

- **Breathe in deeply like a wave coming in.**

- **Breathe out slowly like a wave going out.**

- **Repeat this for one minute and feel how calm you become.**

Draw yourself as a happy, relaxed sea creature floating in the ocean!

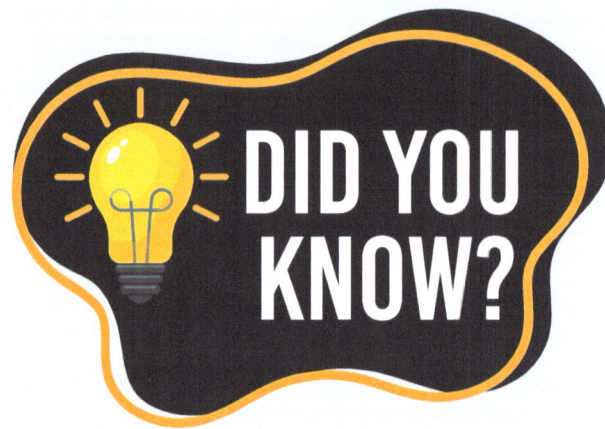

Beach flags help keep you safe by telling you what the ocean conditions are like? Different colors mean different things! Let's learn what each flag means and how to stay safe at the beach!

What do Beach Flags mean?

● Red Flag – High danger! Strong currents and big waves. Stay out of the water!

● Yellow Flag – Medium danger! Waves and currents can be strong. Be extra careful!

● Green Flag – Low danger! The water is calm, but always stay aware.

● Black & White Checkered Flag – Surfing area only! No swimming here.

● Purple Flag – Marine life warning! There may be jellyfish or other sea creatures.

Below are some different kinds of flags to look for on the beach. Choose a color and explain what it means.

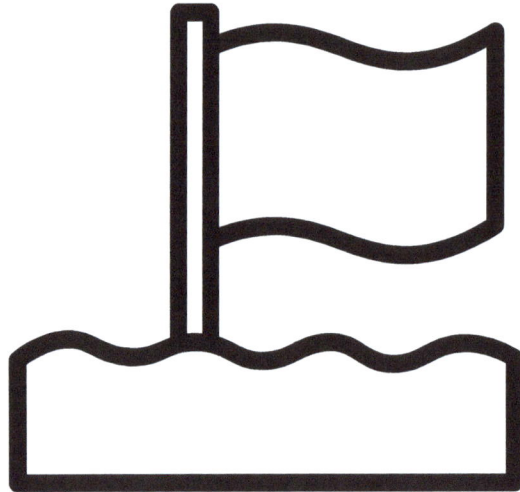

Have fun coloring Shelly the sea turtle:

Have fun coloring this beach scene:

Use all of your favorite colors to brighten up these beach balls:

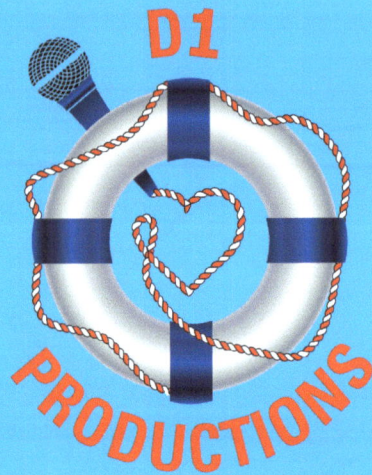